I have been watching
the Great Blue Heron
fish in the cattails...
composing a letter.

TED KOOSER

Either halfway across
or halfway back, he is
stalled between one side
of the day and the other

Ted Kooser

More Than a Local Wonder

Carla Ketner | ILLUSTRATED BY Paula Wallace

University of Nebraska Press

LINCOLN

The University of Nebraska Press is part of a land-grant institution with campuses and programs on the past, present, and future homelands of the Pawnee, Ponca, Otoe-Missouria, Omaha, Dakota, Lakota, Kaw, Cheyenne, and Arapaho Peoples, as well as those of the relocated Ho-Chunk, Sac and Fox, and Iowa Peoples.

Publication of this volume was assisted by the Virginia Faulkner Fund, established in memory of Virginia Faulkner, editor in chief of the University of Nebraska Press.

Library of Congress Control Number: 2023932583

Set and designed in Besley by N. Putens.

For Ted Kooser

In the city of Lincoln, Nebraska, as the 1960s tumbled by, Ted Kooser turned an ordinary refrigerator box into something extraordinary.

Out of that box
soared a great blue heron,

limped an old black dog,
trailed a red fence with no meat on its bones.

Ted sat in that box and wrote
poem
      after poem
           after poem.

While the city slept
Ted painted with words,
portraits of the places and
people he loved.

His molasses-cookie-baking mother,
hat-selling father,
and sister, Judy, made their appearance.
Even his neighbor Mr. Posey
        waddle-floated
            down the dark streets
                    of Ted's poems.

Ted created visions of a man on a bridge
and a house held up by trees,
of his uncle Tubby's magical recliner,
his grandparents' white bungalow,
and his granddaddy's Standard Oil station.

But those poems began even
longer ago, back when he was a
wiry Iowa boy called Teddy.

Teddy was not skilled at sports
and didn't quite fit in,
but he was determined to find his place in the world.

On summer days, while the other kids played ball,
little Teddy gulped ice-cold Nehi grape soda in front of the filling
station his granddaddy ran.
Around him the old farmers turned out tales,
the way their old tractors turned over the rich, dark dirt.

Teddy soaked in those stories.
They grew inside him like seeds in the July heat
and Iowa rains.

And on summer evenings,
while bullfrogs croaked and
cicadas sang,
Teddy perched on his
grandparents' front porch,

listening to yarns his aunts and uncles spun
of a curious cousin in a high-topped buggy,
of floating down the town of Osterdock's flooded streets in boats,
and of a fierce naval battle on the nearby Turkey River.
These were true stories, so they said,
that wrapped around Teddy like a cozy quilt.

One April Teddy received a birthday present.

He saw himself in that book,
in a character named Lentil,
a clever boy who found his way
in a small midwestern town.

the brown map, soldered by tears, red fence, dim garage, a door mat of leaves, against the current, pa, a fat robin, float out into the emptiness, pond, catch an owl, stalk of grass, tiny piece of light, lilac far, wings, a swing, a pearl button, blue buttons, under sails of gingham, shadows, grate

Teddy wanted to be the hero of his own story,
like Lentil,
so one day, when the old men paused for breath,
Teddy swallowed his soda and spun a wild tale of his own,
of his adventures with a talking terrier named Joel.

loosing the trail, season in and season out, map of th
blue woodsmoke, the Big Dipper, la

Teddy was finding his way.
In grade school he wrote his first poem.
In high school poems and stories flew from his pen.

All the while he soaked up the farmers' tales and
took notes of their techniques.
His aunts' and uncles' stories bloomed inside him,
like the iris in spring.

Books filled the empty spaces in
his soul and fired his imagination.

Year after year Ted worked long hours,
but he always made time for writing.
His aunts and uncles and friends,
the gravel roads he walked, the dogs he loved,
and the books he read
all worked their way into Ted's heart and mind
and back out through his stories and poems.

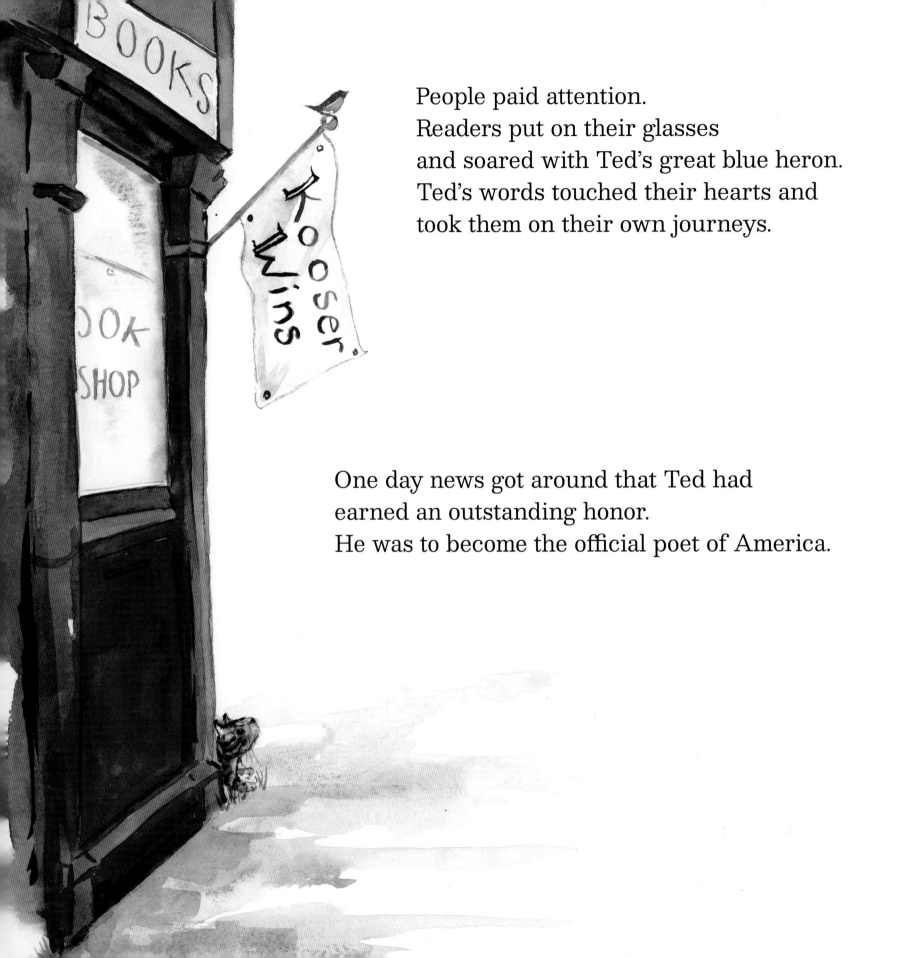

People paid attention.
Readers put on their glasses
and soared with Ted's great blue heron.
Ted's words touched their hearts and
took them on their own journeys.

One day news got around that Ted had
earned an outstanding honor.
He was to become the official poet of America.

The whole town

squeezed into the bookstore to congratulate him.

"You just never know," said Ted that day.
You never can tell what will happen
when a curious little boy
finds stories in the people who surround him
and learns to write poems,

when he fills the empty spaces in his soul
with his own words and finds . . .

You never know

himself.

{ AUTHOR'S NOTE }

Theodore John Kooser was born April 25, 1939, in Ames, Iowa. As a child he was small, quiet, and not athletic and felt that he didn't fit in with his peers. Young Ted found solace in stories, and one specific book, Robert McCloskey's *Lentil*, inspired him to become a writer. Art and writing became Ted's path to success.

As a young man he attended Iowa State University and then taught high school English in a nearby town for a year. Teaching wasn't for Ted, so he and his wife moved to Lincoln, Nebraska, where Ted attended graduate school at the University of Nebraska. They lived in a small apartment, and Ted, needing a private space to write, really did transform a refrigerator box that he found in the alley into an office for himself. While poetry was his true love, he took a job at an insurance company to pay the bills. Every morning he awoke very early and spent several hours reading and writing before he left for work.

When he retired Ted moved to an acreage west of Lincoln, near my hometown. He still wakes before the sun to write—in a *real* office—and takes long walks in the countryside. He is a familiar figure at local cafés and shops.

I first met Ted at the Cattle Bank in Seward, Nebraska, as he was signing copies of *Local Wonders: Seasons in the Bohemian Alps*, his book of stories about the region of Nebraska in which he and I live. I read aloud to my family from that book, on a drive through the very hills Ted had written about. As we listened to his words, we marveled at his gift for capturing what we saw out the car's windows, what we love about our part of Nebraska.

About a year later, in 2004, I opened a bookstore in Seward, and Ted agreed to be the featured guest at my store's grand opening. Then, just days before the grand opening, Ted was named Poet Laureate of the United States. Everyone in Seward County and beyond wanted to congratulate him, and my store was packed with people for the event. We sold out of his books faster than we could say "Ted Kooser is a local wonder." He's been back to the store many times since, and his books top our best-seller lists every year. His gracious presence, poetry, and prose are as much a part of my bookstore as the shelves.

Ted's poetry, essays, and picture books have received many awards, including a Pulitzer Prize for Poetry. As a young boy he discovered the power of stories in his own life. Now his words take his readers on their own journeys, fill their souls, and help them find their places in this world.

Ted Kooser truly is much more than a local wonder.

The University of Nebraska Press
gratefully acknowledges the generous
assistance provided for the publication
of this book by Sarah Biggs-Wudel,
the Cattle Bank & Trust, Gail Clarke,
Chuck and Nancy Peek, Sue Quambusch,
Stephanie E. Rouse, Van and Becky Vahle,
Lynn Overholt Wake, J. P. Wehrman,
and other supporters.

{ REFERENCES }

Works by Ted Kooser Referenced in the Story

POEMS

"Etude," from *Weather Central* (University of Pittsburgh Press, 1994), 3.

"First Snow," from *Sure Signs: New and Selected Poems* (University of Pittsburgh Press, 1980), 4.

"A Man on a Bridge," from *Kindest Regards: New and Selected Poems* (Copper Canyon Press, 2018), 211.

"Selecting a Reader," from *Sure Signs: New and Selected Poems* (University of Pittsburgh Press, 1980), 3.

"Snow Fence," from *Sure Signs: New and Selected Poems* (University of Pittsburgh Press, 1980), 42.

PICTURE BOOKS

House Held Up by Trees (Candlewick Press, 2012).

Mr. Posey's New Glasses (Candlewick Press, 2019).

ESSAY COLLECTIONS

Lights on a Ground of Darkness: An Evocation of a Place and Time (Bison Books, 2009).

Local Wonders: Seasons in the Bohemian Alps (Bison Books, 2002).

Sources of Information about Ted Kooser

Ted Kooser, interview with Carla Ketner, July 16, 2019.

Ted Kooser, *Lights on a Ground of Darkness: An Evocation of a Place and Time* (Bison Books, 2009).

Ted Kooser, *Local Wonders: Seasons in the Bohemian Alps* (Bison Books, 2002).

Luan Pitsch, "Ted Kooser's Bright Lens," The Pilgrimer, February 13, 2015, http://thepilgrimer.com/stories/ted-kooser/ (site discontinued).

Mary K. Stillwell, *The Life and Poetry of Ted Kooser* (Bison Books, 2013).

Snow Fence

The red fence
takes the cold trail
north; no meat
on its ribs,
but neither has it
much to carry.

A Man on a Bridge

Either halfway across or halfway back,
he is stalled between one side of the day
and the other, the dark river, clotted
with foam, flowing down under him,
hands clamped to the cold iron rail
as if he were trying to steer the bridge
upstream, the aluminum paint flaking
under his fingers, his body straining,
so much so that he is unable to turn
to watch a man very much like himself
roll over the bridge in a loaded truck,
and then another man, in a little car
that comes from the other direction,
both of them weighing the bridge down,
weighing him down, too, with their
ordinary errands, while at a standstill,
arms outstretched, he shoves at the rail,
the muscles in his shoulders tight
as he pushes on, against the current.

First Snow

The old black dog comes in one evening
with the first few snowflakes on his back
and falls asleep, throwing his bad leg out
at our excitement. This is the night
when one of us gets to say, as if it were news,
that no two snowflakes are ever alike;
the night when each of us remembers something
snowier. The kitchen is a kindergarten
steamy with stories. The dog gets stiffly up
and limps away, seeking a quiet spot
at the heart of the house. Outside,
in silence, with diamonds in his fur,
the winter night curls round the legs of the trees,
sleepily blinking snowflakes from his lashes.

Selecting a Reader

First, I would have her be beautiful,
and walking carefully up on my poetry
at the loneliest moment of an afternoon,
her hair still damp at the neck
from washing it. She should be wearing
a raincoat, an old one, dirty
from not having money enough for the cleaners.
She will take out her glasses, and there
in the bookstore, she will thumb
over my poems, then put the book back
up on its shelf. She will say to herself,
"For that kind of money, I can get
my raincoat cleaned." And she will.